FIRST LIGHT & EVENTIDE

A DAILY GRATITUDE JOURNAL
by TSH OXENREIDER

Ⰹ

HARVEST HOUSE PUBLISHERS
EUGENE, OREGON

INTRODUCTION

It often feels like there's very little throughout our lives over which we have control. We may spend countless hours dreaming of walking the hallowed halls of a favorite university, decorating our teenage bedrooms with pennants of the team, and angling our transcripts to hedge our bets on acceptance, only to find a rejection letter one day in the mailbox. We may board a plane for a family reunion, only to miss most of the event because of a delayed flight and a missed connection, and then spend the weekend at a nameless airport gate on standby. We see the positive pink line on a test and buy a crib and stroller, only to find out a few months later we'll need to exchange that stroller for a two-seater and squeeze another crib into the corner to match the twins growing inside.

Life never goes according to plan.

Usually, it's the little things that surprise us and keep us on our toes, daily and weekly tossing us curveballs for which we need to adjust our swing and choke up on the bat. We might decide on Sunday afternoon to grill chicken and vegetables for dinner on Wednesday, only to glance out our kitchen window as we marinate the meat and witness a midweek downpour. We study hard for the test, sure the teacher will ask about mitochondria or the Treaty of

Ghent or Brontë's use of gothic symbolism, only to find out something entirely different was on her mind. We may pull up to the drive-through with a hankering for our favorite milkshake, only to find out the machine is broken. We may plant pole beans and peas, only to see the chickens dig up the sprouts for a late-afternoon snack in the garden. (That last one from recent experience.)

If we wake up expecting our days to go exactly how we want, or even how we imagine, we'll walk through life in a constant state of disappointment. It defies logic for us to ask the movements and rhythms of life to be predictable, please and thank you, and yet we crave it all the same. Our bodies long for routine and regimen; we function best with roughly the same sleeping patterns, eating patterns, and traffic patterns. Even if we crave the occasional surprise dessert or whimsical day trip, those changes to our rhythm feel special because they're unusual. If we expect them regularly, they cease to be surprises and, by definition, morph into routines.

We make best-laid plans with good intentions, yet life necessitates an open hand to these ideas. We can't go through our days on the offense, ready to slam away all those unplanned pests like a game of whack-a-mole—we'd be exhausted. (Perhaps we are.) But we also can't dig our heels into the ground, refusing to flex with whatever comes our way, because we'll become brittle, rigid, curmudgeons of life. No one wants to become a curmudgeon.

So what's to be done? Blow around like a leaf in the wind with no agenda to our day whatsoever? Of course not. Be a drill sergeant of our time, trying to force it to bend to our will even when it can't be done? Not possible.

Instead, we plan our days and weeks with good intentions and thoughtful respectability, echoing the ancient words from King Solomon when he said, "We can make our plans, but the LORD determines our steps" (Proverbs 16:9 NLT). Plan, yes. But be open to wherever the day's path leads.

By design we are creatures of habit. We humans crave predictability, so let's give ourselves some where we can. This journal is an invitation for you to incorporate a habit, twice a day, of chronicling your mindset. If the rest of the day is a whirlwind of capricious events, at minimum you've taken charge of how your day begins and ends with a few quiet minutes of intention to jot down what's true, good, and beautiful about life. It only takes a few minutes, but over time, this habit can become the sturdy parapet of your day, protecting you with a hedge of correct thinking and mindful grace for the rest of your waking hours.

BOOKENDS

Picture bookends on a floating shelf and you know why they're there. They hold up what's in between—usually a row of books. You move them to fit what they support, but otherwise, they're sturdy, they're simple, and their existence allows books to be reachable for their reader. Without them, libraries would be a mess.

Our days have bookends too. Every morning and evening we begin and end

Sometimes, if you stand on the bottom rail of a bridge and lean over to watch the river slipping slowly away beneath you, you will suddenly know everything there is to be known.

—A.A. MILNE

our days, and in that time most of us perform a predictable routine we likely don't even notice. The evening begins a cycle of sleep necessary for bodily restoration so we can function during our next cycle of being awake. Again and again, we repeat this rhythm so we can do it again the next day, the next, and the next. Our quality and quantity of sleep changes from night to night, but otherwise we perform the same basic task: horizontal on the bed, eyes closed, brain engaged in cycles of REM.

Anything goes during the waking hours between our times of sleep, and no one has the same experience. Many of us don't even have the same experience from day to day in our own individual lives—if you've got kids, an unpredictable job, or an otherwise hefty stack of plates to spin, you already know how different one day is from the next. One day you're committed to a deluge of meetings at the office; the next day you're the family taxi driver delivering passengers to soccer practice and friend hangouts between your runs to the post office and grocery store.

If we have an ever-changing, reactive posture to our days, desperately grasping for something sturdy and secure, it's no wonder if we collapse into bed exhausted. Our minds, bodies, and souls yearn for restoration.

No matter the kinds of days we have, daily bookends serve as ramparts to give us something sturdy when most everything else feels as flimsy as a leaf in the wind. Even on those days when our routines are mercifully as they should be, bookends still help make sure they remain that way. They help keep things where they belong.

So what are these morning and evening bookends?

You likely already have them in some fashion. You wake up to your alarm, go to the bathroom, check your phone while the coffee brews, let the dog out in the backyard, and take your meds. When you scroll your phone while you wait for the coffee, you likely peruse the same apps in the same order, hopping from the weather, to your calendar, to your email, to your social media flavor of choice. In the evening, you might sit in "your" spot on the couch and watch a few episodes of the current show you're bingeing, then gather dirty dishes to the dishwasher and hit the start button, brush your teeth (starting with the same teeth and proceeding to the rest of your mouth in the same order), apply concoctions and potions of choice to your body, arrange the familiar items on your nightstand just-so, and then crack open your current book and read a few pages before falling asleep.

> *It is not enough to be busy. So are the ants. The question is: What are we busy about?*
> —HENRY DAVID THOREAU

Your version of bookends has its own ingredients, but the idea is common— we humans have predictable routines to help our bodies do what they have to do in order to function: go to sleep and wake up.

If you already perform a series of rhythmic routines for your morning and evening bookends, why not make them intentional? Why not infuse a proactive posture to how you begin and end your days in order to balance the reactive posture you may have to take during the hours in-between?

Each of your bookends must be customized to your unique stage of life (it's madness bordering on insanity to suggest the mother of a newborn should begin her day with an hour of reading before the sun rises). Therefore, I won't make any broad brushstroke declarations about the "best" ingredients to comprise your bookends, though generally speaking, there are a few tried-and-true favorites: coffee, reading, prayer, exercise, to-do lists, showering, teeth-brushing, and the like. Likewise, the size of bookends depends entirely on a person's reality: A retired empty nester could spend two hours in their leisurely morning bookend while a working parent of school-age children might devote ten minutes to theirs, max.

In other words, there's no *one* correct way to use the concept of bookends to begin and end a day. We already know this because we live it. It's obvious. But it bears mentioning because the well-intentioned, idealistic among us far too often pine for routines that simply aren't possible, which can lead us to kicking ourselves if we don't run three miles every morning or if we fall asleep every time we crack open the novel on the nightstand. We do best when we acknowledge what's possible, remember that life changes frequently, and embrace a proactive posture for that which we can control.

This leads us to the benefit this journal can provide.

EXAMEN

Saint Ignatius of Loyola was a sixteenth-century Spanish theologian and mystic and the founder of the Society of Jesus, colloquially known as the Jesuits. A soldier in the military, he had ambitious career plans in politics and public service before he was badly injured by a French cannonball. During his convalescence, he experienced a dramatic conversion, embarked on a spiritual pilgrimage, and ultimately founded a faith-filled society that asked its members to participate in a monthlong program of introspective challenges, or Spiritual Exercises. Then these disciples were to reimmerse themselves in the culture around them and continue "finding God in all things" there.

Ultimately this form of spiritual training, with its pattern of meditation and contemplation in order to hear from God throughout the ins and outs of a day, led to a central practice known as the Examination of Consciousness, or simply "Examen." Five hundred years later, people all over the world still embark in this daily practice, both christened Jesuits who have taken official vows, and everyday folks like the rest of us.

In short, Examen is a daily time of prayer when a person expresses gratitude to God, reflects on the day and notices God's hand in it, and asks for guidance about what's next. This practice was so essential to Ignatius that he directed his Jesuits to practice the Examen twice daily. It may seem like a simple concept to us today, but Examen became the

> *The only man who never makes mistakes is the man who never does anything.*
> —THEODORE ROOSEVELT

hallmark of Ignatius's Spiritual Exercises as a way of engaging in the world and noticing God in the everyday.

His military background helped him provide a tight, structured framework for his followers, and while we certainly don't need to embody a dogmatic formation designed for soldiers in boot camp, we would still be wise to recognize his application of order to the important, contemplative parts of our day.

Examen is usually associated with the evening, as a way to close out the day. It traditionally consists of five steps that lead a person to notice God's

presence, repent, and plan for the next day. Mark Thibodeaux, a Jesuit spir-
itual director, uses the mnemonic of Relish, Request, Review, Repent, and Resolve to help remember these steps.[1] A traditional evening Examen is indeed a robust method of ending a day, and a time-tested one at that. Yet you can customize the tradition so that it best suits your particular life stage, situation, and temperament. You can also tap into the wisdom of Examen in the morning to bookend your day with contemplation and awareness to help you spend your waking hours well.

How do you do this? This journal is a good place to start.

> *Tell me to what you pay attention and I will tell you who you are.*
>
> —JOSE ORTEGA Y GASSET

1. Mark E. Thibodeaux, *Reimagining the Ignatian Examen: Fresh Ways to Pray from Your Day* (Chicago: Loyola Press, 2015), xi.

IF YOU WANT TO BUILD A SHIP,
DON'T DRUM UP THE MEN TO GATHER
WOOD, DIVIDE THE WORK, AND GIVE
ORDERS. INSTEAD, TEACH THEM TO YEARN
FOR THE VAST AND ENDLESS SEA.

—*Antoine de Saint-Exupéry*

SIX QUESTIONS

After several years of adjusting, tweaking, and making habits in my morning and evening routines, I've settled on six questions to form my own Examen-like rhythm—three for the morning, three for the evening. Taking roughly five minutes for each session, ten tops, prayerfully contemplating these six questions has been an essential ingredient in my bookends.

In the morning I ask these questions:

1. **GRATITUDE**—*What three things am I thankful for this morning?*

2. **GREATER TRUTH**—*What is one absolutely true thing about myself or God?*

3. **GOOD-DAY GRACE**—*What is one thing in my control that would make this day a good one?*

And in the evening, I ask these questions:

1. **GRATITUDE**—*What are three more things I am thankful for this evening?*

2. **GAFFES**—*What one thing would have made today better?*

3. **GOOD-NIGHT GIFT**—*What one thing can I ask for God's help with?*

Let's consider each of these short but prayerful questions and explore why they are so helpful.

GRATITUDE

The science is there, and so is the anecdotal evidence: A regular habit of practicing gratitude makes us happier and healthier. When we purposely notice the particular good things in life, we combat the negativity bias that so often assaults our human tendency to focus on the bad and forget the good. We complain less, which makes us more enjoyable to be around. When we focus better on what's working instead of what's not, we're more aware of the abundance of blessings around us and less focused on what's missing.

By also specifically writing down what we're grateful for, we're participating in the practice of engaging the mind and body with noticing the good, and are also therefore better setting ourselves up for even more benefits. Studies have shown that people who keep gratitude journals also exercise more regularly and experience fewer negative physical symptoms, feel better about their lives as a whole, are more optimistic, are more likely to make progress toward important personal goals, report higher levels of alertness and energy, sense agreater feeling of connection to others, and even sleep better.[2] The benefits of gratitude are astronomical, and there are no downsides.

I've also found it's essential to keep my gratitude focus as granular and specific as possible. It's not enough for me to be thankful for the miraculous discovery of brewed coffee—I need to be thankful for the particular roast of the pour in my mug,

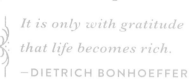

It is only with gratitude that life becomes rich.
—DIETRICH BONHOEFFER

or the color of the mug itself, or the memory of where and when I procured the mug. Starting and ending the day with three particular things I'm thankful for—for a total of six per day—means I can afford to be specific. And we *should* be specific because it enhances our gratitude. We're more aware of the tiny, otherwise commonplace blessings of our lives.

GREATER TRUTH

We humans far too often tinker with ideas and thoughts about ourselves or God (or both) that simply aren't true. Whether they are ideas about our days ("The things I have to do today are too much for me to handle;" "Nothing I do today will be noticed or even matter") or core thoughts about who we are ("I'm too lazy to get anything done") or who God is ("God isn't really here"), our minds wage a battle between lies and truth even when we're unaware. We could be sitting at

---

2. Robert Emmons, "Gratitude and Well-Being," https://emmons.faculty.ucdavis.edu /gratitude-and-well-being/.

the breakfast table nursing a bowl of granola and mentally engaging in a skirmish of good and evil with nary a notice.

It's essential to begin each day remembering what's true. It might be something timeless and cosmically mind-blowing, like "The God of the universe knows me," or something smaller but still significant, like "My friends like me for who I am." Both types of truths are important.

By writing down one statement of truth every morning, you're acknowledging that there is a core rightness about the world and who you are, even if it doesn't feel like it. Truth doesn't depend on how you feel. Truth simply *is*.

It is the LORD who goes before you. He will be with you; he will not fail you or forsake you. Do not fear or be dismayed.

—DEUTERONOMY 31:8

Often my one morning truth is simply "I am a beloved child of God, able to do hard things." Other times it's "God will give me exactly what I need to accomplish what's necessary today." Both are things I forget far more often than I care to admit, and yet they're truths I can't embrace often enough.

GOOD-DAY GRACE

We have far more agency over our days than we give ourselves credit for. It's easy to take a victim posture about what's on our plates for the day, but in reality, our free will gives us lots of control. Ultimately, God is in authority—again, Solomon reminds us of this when he says, "We can make our plans, but the LORD determines our steps" (Proverbs 16:9 NLT)—but we still must go about the day with a plan.

There's no need to overwhelm ourselves with a 27-item to-do list, but as people made to work, we are most likely able to exercise agency over at least one thing each day. By naming one thing that, through God's grace, would make our day a good one, we're acknowledging our ability to make the most of the gift of another day.

Now, notice that this thing you name must be something in *your* control. It's not helpful to say, "Today will be good if Mrs. Adams cancels the math test," or "Today will be good if there are donuts in the break room," because this is simply wishful thinking. We're not rubbing the side of a genie's lamp when we name our good-day grace. When we write down one thing in our control about today, we're admitting to ourselves that, with God's grace, we can usually do something about our day.

Your good-day grace could be specifically about your to-do list, such as "Today will be good if I go on an afternoon walk" or "Today will be good if I pay the electric bill," but it can also be about your state of mind—"Today will be good if I pause for three seconds before responding to my tantrum-throwing toddler" is a good example. No matter your grace for the day, it must be within your control.

GAFFES

It might seem strange that I'd suggest spending a minute or two each evening taking note of what went wrong. But failure is not only part of life, we can also allow it to be one of our greatest teachers. The spoiler alert of each day is that things won't go 100 percent as planned. It might be a near-perfect day,

*Plan for what
is difficult while
it is easy.*

—SUN TZU

but there will still be a bird that poops on your newly washed car or a dinner that could be better seasoned. This is just life on this side of heaven, and it's okay.

By taking time to acknowledge your day's imperfections, you're embracing the idea that it's okay when things don't go exactly as planned. You're combating the enemy known as perfectionism.

Your day's gaffe could be relatively insignificant ("I didn't go to the gym like I wanted") or something a bit more substantial ("My pitch at work fell through and the client didn't accept my offer"), but by participating in the act of naming it, we're giving it less power over our attitude. We're embracing the truth that life isn't perfect, and that's okay. God-willing we have another chance with a new day tomorrow.

GOOD-NIGHT GIFT

This brings us to the final question of the evening: What's one thing I can ask for God's help with? Before I turn out the light and fall asleep, what's one thing I need? God is the giver of all good things, and we know from experience today that we'll continue to need more grace tomorrow. What's one specific need?

It might be "more patience with my kids," "more self-control around sugar," or "more tolerance around people different from me." It may be something specific about tomorrow like "wisdom in how to engage in that upcoming difficult conversation" or "concentration and memory during my history quiz." It may very well be simply "a good night of sound sleep"—that's often my good-night gift.

Whatever it is, writing down a specific good-night gift reminds us of our posture as humans: We are dependent on God, a loving Father who wants to give good things to his children.

Finish each day and be done with it. You have done what you could. . . . Tomorrow is a new day.

—RALPH WALDO EMERSON

THE BENEFIT OF ADDING TIMELESS WISDOM

Our cultural timeline is full of brilliant women and men who were sojourners just like ourselves, figuring out life along the way. Thankfully, some of them wrote down tidbits of truth to remind us of what's most important. We would do well to take heed to these sages, to listen to enduring wisdom that remains true today. G.K. Chesterton called tradition "the democracy of the dead," which he said means "giving a vote to the most obscure of all classes: our ancestors."[3] The sagacious wisdom written for posterity by our cultural ancestors has stood the test of time because there is at least an element of truth in it, and we would do well to heed it.

This journal includes wisdom from these traditional thinkers, words we need to remember and apply to our daily lives. In a world that's quick to shun the old and praise the new, it's good to ground our bookends in reminders of ideas that have lasted.

3. "Tradition Is the Democracy of the Dead." The Society of G.K. Chesterton, April 29, 2012. https://www.chesterton.org/democracy-of-the-dead/.

BEST PRACTICES

To incorporate this journal into your morning and evening bookends, keep it accessible: Your nightstand is an obvious choice. Keep a pen or pencil at the ready, and until it's part of your natural routine, you might want to add a notification reminder in your device or a simple sticky note on your lamp.

Once writing in this journal becomes a daily habit, answering these six questions will probably take you no more than ten minutes, yet they'll become an essential part of your day's scaffolding. They will help you flesh out your modern-day Examen and give you a deeply Ignatian practice, time tested, for your ordinary life.

KNOWING OTHERS IS INTELLIGENCE;
KNOWING YOURSELF IS TRUE WISDOM.
MASTERING OTHERS IS STRENGTH;
MASTERING YOURSELF IS TRUE POWER.

—*Lao Tzu*

*Yesterday is gone. Tomorrow has not
yet come. We have only today. Let us begin.*
—SAINT TERESA OF CALCUTTA

DAILY
ENTRIES

MORNING

GRATITUDE: *What three things am I thankful for this morning?*

1. _____
2. _____
3. _____

GREATER TRUTH: *What is one absolutely true thing about myself or God?*

_____
_____
_____
_____
_____

GOOD-DAY GRACE: *What is one thing in my control that would make this day a good one?*

_____
_____
_____
_____

EVENING

All we have to decide is what to do with the time that is given us.

—J.R.R. TOLKIEN

GRATITUDE: *What are three more things I am thankful for this evening?*

1. _____
2. _____
3. _____

GAFFES: *What one thing would have made today better?*

_____
_____
_____
_____
_____

GOOD-NIGHT GIFT: *What one thing can I ask for God's help with?*

_____
_____
_____
_____
_____

MORNING

GRATITUDE: *What three things am I thankful for this morning?*

1. _____
2. _____
3. _____

GREATER TRUTH: *What is one absolutely true thing about myself or God?*

_____
_____
_____
_____
_____

GOOD-DAY GRACE: *What is one thing in my control that would make this day a good one?*

_____
_____
_____
_____

EVENING

When we cannot pray as we would, it is good to pray as we can.
—CHARLES SPURGEON

GRATITUDE: *What are three more things I am thankful for this evening?*

1. _____
2. _____
3. _____

GAFFES: *What one thing would have made today better?*

_____
_____
_____
_____
_____

GOOD-NIGHT GIFT: *What one thing can I ask for God's help with?*

_____
_____
_____
_____

MORNING

GRATITUDE: *What three things am I thankful for this morning?*

1. _____
2. _____
3. _____

GREATER TRUTH: *What is one absolutely true thing about myself or God?*

_____
_____
_____
_____
_____

GOOD-DAY GRACE: *What is one thing in my control that would make this day a good one?*

_____
_____
_____
_____
_____

EVENING

GRATITUDE: *What are three more things I am thankful for this evening?*

1. _____
2. _____
3. _____

GAFFES: *What one thing would have made today better?*

_____

_____

_____

_____

GOOD-NIGHT GIFT: *What one thing can I ask for God's help with?*

_____

_____

_____

_____

_____

MORNING

GRATITUDE: *What three things am I thankful for this morning?*

1. _____
2. _____
3. _____

GREATER TRUTH: *What is one absolutely true thing about myself or God?*

_____
_____
_____
_____
_____

GOOD-DAY GRACE: *What is one thing in my control that would make this day a good one?*

_____
_____
_____
_____

EVENING

We know that in all things God works for the good of those who love
him, who have been called according to his purpose.

—ROMANS 8:28 NIV

GRATITUDE: *What are three more things I am thankful for this evening?*

1. _____
2. _____
3. _____

GAFFES: *What one thing would have made today better?*

_____
_____
_____
_____
_____

GOOD-NIGHT GIFT: *What one thing can I ask for God's help with?*

_____
_____
_____
_____
_____

MORNING

DAY 5

__/__/__

GRATITUDE: *What three things am I thankful for this morning?*

1. _____
2. _____
3. _____

GREATER TRUTH: *What is one absolutely true thing about myself or God?*

_____
_____
_____
_____
_____

GOOD-DAY GRACE: *What is one thing in my control that would make this day a good one?*

_____
_____
_____
_____

EVENING

The man who moves a mountain begins by carrying away small stones.

—CONFUCIUS

GRATITUDE: *What are three more things I am thankful for this evening?*

1. _____
2. _____
3. _____

GAFFES: *What one thing would have made today better?*

_____
_____
_____
_____
_____

GOOD-NIGHT GIFT: *What one thing can I ask for God's help with?*

_____
_____
_____
_____
_____

MORNING

DAY 6

__/__/__

GRATITUDE: *What three things am I thankful for this morning?*

1. _____
2. _____
3. _____

GREATER TRUTH: *What is one absolutely true thing about myself or God?*

_____

_____

_____

_____

GOOD-DAY GRACE: *What is one thing in my control that would make this day a good one?*

_____

_____

_____

_____

EVENING

*Most of our life is unimportant, filled with trivial things
from morning till night. But when it is transformed by love it
is of interest even to the angels.*

—DOROTHY DAY

GRATITUDE: *What are three more things I am thankful for this evening?*

1. _____
2. _____
3. _____

GAFFES: *What one thing would have made today better?*

_____
_____
_____
_____
_____

GOOD-NIGHT GIFT: *What one thing can I ask for God's help with?*

_____
_____
_____
_____
_____

MORNING

GRATITUDE: *What three things am I thankful for this morning?*

1. _____
2. _____
3. _____

GREATER TRUTH: *What is one absolutely true thing about myself or God?*

_____
_____
_____
_____

GOOD-DAY GRACE: *What is one thing in my control that would make this day a good one?*

_____
_____
_____
_____

EVENING

The whole earth is a living icon of the face of God.
—SAINT JOHN OF DAMASCUS

GRATITUDE: *What are three more things I am thankful for this evening?*

1. _____
2. _____
3. _____

GAFFES: *What one thing would have made today better?*

_____
_____
_____
_____
_____

GOOD-NIGHT GIFT: *What one thing can I ask for God's help with?*

_____
_____
_____
_____
_____

MORNING

GRATITUDE: *What three things am I thankful for this morning?*

    1. _____

    2. _____

    3. _____

GREATER TRUTH: *What is one absolutely true thing about myself or God?*

_____

_____

_____

_____

_____

GOOD-DAY GRACE: *What is one thing in my control that would make this day a good one?*

_____

_____

_____

_____

_____

EVENING

Pay attention to where you are going because without
meaning you might get nowhere.

—A.A. MILNE

GRATITUDE: *What are three more things I am thankful for this evening?*

1. _____
2. _____
3. _____

GAFFES: *What one thing would have made today better?*

_____
_____
_____
_____
_____

GOOD-NIGHT GIFT: *What one thing can I ask for God's help with?*

_____
_____
_____
_____
_____

MORNING

GRATITUDE: *What three things am I thankful for this morning?*

1. _____
2. _____
3. _____

GREATER TRUTH: *What is one absolutely true thing about myself or God?*

_____

_____

_____

_____

GOOD-DAY GRACE: *What is one thing in my control that would make this day a good one?*

_____

_____

_____

_____

EVENING

Small opportunities are often the beginning of great enterprises.
—DEMOSTHENES

GRATITUDE: *What are three more things I am thankful for this evening?*

1. _____
2. _____
3. _____

GAFFES: *What one thing would have made today better?*

_____
_____
_____
_____
_____

GOOD-NIGHT GIFT: *What one thing can I ask for God's help with?*

_____
_____
_____
_____
_____

MORNING

GRATITUDE: *What three things am I thankful for this morning?*

1. _____
2. _____
3. _____

GREATER TRUTH: *What is one absolutely true thing about myself or God?*

_____
_____
_____
_____
_____

GOOD-DAY GRACE: *What is one thing in my control that would make this day a good one?*

_____
_____
_____
_____

EVENING

GRATITUDE: *What are three more things I am thankful for this evening?*

1. _____
2. _____
3. _____

GAFFES: *What one thing would have made today better?*

_____
_____
_____
_____
_____

GOOD-NIGHT GIFT: *What one thing can I ask for God's help with?*

_____
_____
_____
_____

MORNING

GRATITUDE: *What three things am I thankful for this morning?*

    1. _____

    2. _____

    3. _____

GREATER TRUTH: *What is one absolutely true thing about myself or God?*

_____

_____

_____

_____

GOOD-DAY GRACE: *What is one thing in my control that would make this day a good one?*

_____

_____

_____

_____

EVENING

*We cannot do great deeds . . . unless we are willing
to do the small things that make up the sum of greatness.*

—THEODORE ROOSEVELT

GRATITUDE: *What are three more things I am thankful for this evening?*

1. _____
2. _____
3. _____

GAFFES: *What one thing would have made today better?*

_____
_____
_____
_____

GOOD-NIGHT GIFT: *What one thing can I ask for God's help with?*

_____
_____
_____
_____

MORNING

DAY 12

__/__/__

GRATITUDE: *What three things am I thankful for this morning?*

1. _____
2. _____
3. _____

GREATER TRUTH: *What is one absolutely true thing about myself or God?*

_____
_____
_____
_____
_____

GOOD-DAY GRACE: *What is one thing in my control that would make this day a good one?*

_____
_____
_____
_____

EVENING

I alone cannot change the world, but I can cast
a stone across the waters to create many ripples.

— SAINT TERESA OF CALCUTTA

GRATITUDE: *What are three more things I am thankful for this evening?*

1. _____
2. _____
3. _____

GAFFES: *What one thing would have made today better?*

_____
_____
_____
_____
_____

GOOD-NIGHT GIFT: *What one thing can I ask for God's help with?*

_____
_____
_____
_____
_____

MORNING

GRATITUDE: *What three things am I thankful for this morning?*

1. _____
2. _____
3. _____

GREATER TRUTH: *What is one absolutely true thing about myself or God?*

_____
_____
_____
_____

GOOD-DAY GRACE: *What is one thing in my control that would make this day a good one?*

_____
_____
_____
_____

EVENING

Creativity takes courage.
—HENRI MATISSE

GRATITUDE: *What are three more things I am thankful for this evening?*

1. _____
2. _____
3. _____

GAFFES: *What one thing would have made today better?*

_____
_____
_____
_____
_____

GOOD-NIGHT GIFT: *What one thing can I ask for God's help with?*

_____
_____
_____
_____

MORNING

GRATITUDE: *What three things am I thankful for this morning?*

1. _____
2. _____
3. _____

GREATER TRUTH: *What is one absolutely true thing about myself or God?*

_____
_____
_____
_____
_____

GOOD-DAY GRACE: *What is one thing in my control that would make this day a good one?*

_____
_____
_____

EVENING

There are two ways to get enough. One is to continue to accumulate more and more. The other is to desire less.

—G.K. CHESTERTON

GRATITUDE: *What are three more things I am thankful for this evening?*

1. _____
2. _____
3. _____

GAFFES: *What one thing would have made today better?*

_____
_____
_____
_____
_____

GOOD-NIGHT GIFT: *What one thing can I ask for God's help with?*

_____
_____
_____
_____
_____

MORNING

GRATITUDE: *What three things am I thankful for this morning?*

1. _____
2. _____
3. _____

GREATER TRUTH: *What is one absolutely true thing about myself or God?*

_____
_____
_____
_____
_____

GOOD-DAY GRACE: *What is one thing in my control that would make this day a good one?*

_____
_____
_____
_____

EVENING

Labor to keep alive in your breast that
little spark of celestial fire called conscience.
—GEORGE WASHINGTON

GRATITUDE: *What are three more things I am thankful for this evening?*

1. _____
2. _____
3. _____

GAFFES: *What one thing would have made today better?*

_____
_____
_____
_____
_____

GOOD-NIGHT GIFT: *What one thing can I ask for God's help with?*

_____
_____
_____
_____
_____

MORNING

GRATITUDE: *What three things am I thankful for this morning?*

1. _____
2. _____
3. _____

GREATER TRUTH: *What is one absolutely true thing about myself or God?*

_____

_____

_____

_____

_____

GOOD-DAY GRACE: *What is one thing in my control that would make this day a good one?*

_____

_____

_____

_____

EVENING

Do not spoil what you have by desiring what you have not; remember that
what you now have was once among the things you only hoped for.

—EPICURUS

GRATITUDE: *What are three more things I am thankful for this evening?*

1. _____
2. _____
3. _____

GAFFES: *What one thing would have made today better?*

_____
_____
_____
_____

GOOD-NIGHT GIFT: *What one thing can I ask for God's help with?*

_____
_____
_____
_____

MORNING

DAY 17

—/—/—

GRATITUDE: *What three things am I thankful for this morning?*

1. _____
2. _____
3. _____

GREATER TRUTH: *What is one absolutely true thing about myself or God?*

_____

_____

_____

_____

_____

GOOD-DAY GRACE: *What is one thing in my control that would make this day a good one?*

_____

_____

_____

_____

_____

EVENING

Be who God meant you to be and you will set the world on fire.
—SAINT CATHERINE OF SIENA

GRATITUDE: *What are three more things I am thankful for this evening?*

1. _____
2. _____
3. _____

GAFFES: *What one thing would have made today better?*

_____
_____
_____
_____
_____

GOOD-NIGHT GIFT: *What one thing can I ask for God's help with?*

_____
_____
_____
_____
_____

MORNING

GRATITUDE: *What three things am I thankful for this morning?*

1. _____
2. _____
3. _____

GREATER TRUTH: *What is one absolutely true thing about myself or God?*

_____
_____
_____
_____
_____

GOOD-DAY GRACE: *What is one thing in my control that would make this day a good one?*

_____
_____
_____
_____

EVENING

*If we wait for the moment when
everything . . . is ready, we shall never begin.*

—IVAN TURGENEV

GRATITUDE: *What are three more things I am thankful for this evening?*

1. _____
2. _____
3. _____

GAFFES: *What one thing would have made today better?*

_____
_____
_____
_____
_____

GOOD-NIGHT GIFT: *What one thing can I ask for God's help with?*

_____
_____
_____
_____
_____

MORNING

GRATITUDE: *What three things am I thankful for this morning?*

1. _____
2. _____
3. _____

GREATER TRUTH: *What is one absolutely true thing about myself or God?*

_____
_____
_____
_____
_____

GOOD-DAY GRACE: *What is one thing in my control that would make this day a good one?*

_____
_____
_____
_____

EVENING

May you be strengthened with all power, according to his glorious might, for all endurance and patience with joy.

—COLOSSIANS 1:11 HCSB

GRATITUDE: *What are three more things I am thankful for this evening?*

1. _____
2. _____
3. _____

GAFFES: *What one thing would have made today better?*

_____
_____
_____
_____
_____

GOOD-NIGHT GIFT: *What one thing can I ask for God's help with?*

_____
_____
_____
_____

MORNING

GRATITUDE: *What three things am I thankful for this morning?*

1. _____
2. _____
3. _____

GREATER TRUTH: *What is one absolutely true thing about myself or God?*

_____
_____
_____
_____

GOOD-DAY GRACE: *What is one thing in my control that would make this day a good one?*

_____
_____
_____
_____

EVENING

Even in a world that's being shipwrecked, remain brave and strong.
—SAINT HILDEGARD OF BINGEN

GRATITUDE: *What are three more things I am thankful for this evening?*

1. _____
2. _____
3. _____

GAFFES: *What one thing would have made today better?*

_____
_____
_____
_____
_____

GOOD-NIGHT GIFT: *What one thing can I ask for God's help with?*

_____
_____
_____
_____
_____

MORNING

GRATITUDE: *What three things am I thankful for this morning?*

1. _____
2. _____
3. _____

GREATER TRUTH: *What is one absolutely true thing about myself or God?*

_____
_____
_____
_____
_____

GOOD-DAY GRACE: *What is one thing in my control that would make this day a good one?*

_____
_____
_____
_____

EVENING

GRATITUDE: *What are three more things I am thankful for this evening?*

1. _____
2. _____
3. _____

GAFFES: *What one thing would have made today better?*

_____
_____
_____
_____
_____

GOOD-NIGHT GIFT: *What one thing can I ask for God's help with?*

_____
_____
_____
_____

MORNING

DAY 22

__/__/__

GRATITUDE: *What three things am I thankful for this morning?*

1. _____
2. _____
3. _____

GREATER TRUTH: *What is one absolutely true thing about myself or God?*

_____

_____

_____

_____

_____

GOOD-DAY GRACE: *What is one thing in my control that would make this day a good one?*

_____

_____

_____

_____

EVENING

Nothing should be more highly prized than the value of each day.

—GOETHE

GRATITUDE: *What are three more things I am thankful for this evening?*

1. _____
2. _____
3. _____

GAFFES: *What one thing would have made today better?*

_____
_____
_____
_____
_____

GOOD-NIGHT GIFT: *What one thing can I ask for God's help with?*

_____
_____
_____
_____
_____

MORNING

GRATITUDE: *What three things am I thankful for this morning?*

1. _____
2. _____
3. _____

GREATER TRUTH: *What is one absolutely true thing about myself or God?*

_____

_____

_____

_____

GOOD-DAY GRACE: *What is one thing in my control that would make this day a good one?*

_____

_____

_____

_____

EVENING

GRATITUDE: *What are three more things I am thankful for this evening?*

1. _____
2. _____
3. _____

GAFFES: *What one thing would have made today better?*

_____
_____
_____
_____
_____

GOOD-NIGHT GIFT: *What one thing can I ask for God's help with?*

_____
_____
_____
_____
_____

MORNING

GRATITUDE: *What three things am I thankful for this morning?*

1. _____
2. _____
3. _____

GREATER TRUTH: *What is one absolutely true thing about myself or God?*

_____
_____
_____
_____
_____

GOOD-DAY GRACE: *What is one thing in my control that would make this day a good one?*

_____
_____
_____
_____
_____

EVENING

GRATITUDE: *What are three more things I am thankful for this evening?*

1. _____
2. _____
3. _____

GAFFES: *What one thing would have made today better?*

_____
_____
_____
_____

GOOD-NIGHT GIFT: *What one thing can I ask for God's help with?*

_____
_____
_____
_____

MORNING

GRATITUDE: *What three things am I thankful for this morning?*

1. _____
2. _____
3. _____

GREATER TRUTH: *What is one absolutely true thing about myself or God?*

_____
_____
_____
_____
_____

GOOD-DAY GRACE: *What is one thing in my control that would make this day a good one?*

_____
_____
_____
_____

EVENING

GRATITUDE: *What are three more things I am thankful for this evening?*

1. _____
2. _____
3. _____

GAFFES: *What one thing would have made today better?*

_____

_____

_____

_____

_____

GOOD-NIGHT GIFT: *What one thing can I ask for God's help with?*

_____

_____

_____

_____

_____

_____

MORNING

GRATITUDE: *What three things am I thankful for this morning?*

1. _____
2. _____
3. _____

GREATER TRUTH: *What is one absolutely true thing about myself or God?*

_____
_____
_____
_____
_____

GOOD-DAY GRACE: *What is one thing in my control that would make this day a good one?*

_____
_____
_____
_____

EVENING

Leisure . . . is not the privilege of those who can afford to take time; it is the
virtue of those who give to everything they do the time it deserves to take.
—DAVID STEINDL-RAST

GRATITUDE: *What are three more things I am thankful for this evening?*

1. _____
2. _____
3. _____

GAFFES: *What one thing would have made today better?*

_____
_____
_____
_____
_____

GOOD-NIGHT GIFT: *What one thing can I ask for God's help with?*

_____
_____
_____
_____

MORNING

DAY 27

__/__/__

GRATITUDE: *What three things am I thankful for this morning?*

1. _____
2. _____
3. _____

GREATER TRUTH: *What is one absolutely true thing about myself or God?*

_____

_____

_____

_____

GOOD-DAY GRACE: *What is one thing in my control that would make this day a good one?*

_____

_____

_____

_____

EVENING

*We have to do with the past only as we can make
it useful to the present and the future.*

—FREDERICK DOUGLASS

GRATITUDE: *What are three more things I am thankful for this evening?*

1. _____
2. _____
3. _____

GAFFES: *What one thing would have made today better?*

_____

_____

_____

_____

_____

GOOD-NIGHT GIFT: *What one thing can I ask for God's help with?*

_____

_____

_____

_____

_____

MORNING

GRATITUDE: *What three things am I thankful for this morning?*

1. _____
2. _____
3. _____

GREATER TRUTH: *What is one absolutely true thing about myself or God?*

_____
_____
_____
_____
_____

GOOD-DAY GRACE: *What is one thing in my control that would make this day a good one?*

_____
_____
_____
_____
_____

EVENING

Courage, hard work, self-mastery, and intelligent
effort are all essential to successful life.
—THEODORE ROOSEVELT

GRATITUDE: *What are three more things I am thankful for this evening?*

1. _____
2. _____
3. _____

GAFFES: *What one thing would have made today better?*

_____
_____
_____
_____
_____

GOOD-NIGHT GIFT: *What one thing can I ask for God's help with?*

_____
_____
_____
_____

MORNING

DAY 29

__/__/__

GRATITUDE: *What three things am I thankful for this morning?*

    1. _____
    2. _____
    3. _____

GREATER TRUTH: *What is one absolutely true thing about myself or God?*

_____
_____
_____
_____
_____

GOOD-DAY GRACE: *What is one thing in my control that would make this day a good one?*

_____
_____
_____
_____
_____

EVENING

Peace I leave with you; my peace I give to you. I do not give to you as the world gives. Do not let your hearts be troubled, and do not let them be afraid.

—JOHN 14:27

GRATITUDE: *What are three more things I am thankful for this evening?*

1. _____
2. _____
3. _____

GAFFES: *What one thing would have made today better?*

_____
_____
_____
_____
_____

GOOD-NIGHT GIFT: *What one thing can I ask for God's help with?*

_____
_____
_____
_____

MORNING

GRATITUDE: *What three things am I thankful for this morning?*

1. _____
2. _____
3. _____

GREATER TRUTH: *What is one absolutely true thing about myself or God?*

_____
_____
_____
_____
_____

GOOD-DAY GRACE: *What is one thing in my control that would make this day a good one?*

_____
_____
_____
_____

EVENING

GRATITUDE: *What are three more things I am thankful for this evening?*

1. _____
2. _____
3. _____

GAFFES: *What one thing would have made today better?*

_____
_____
_____
_____
_____

GOOD-NIGHT GIFT: *What one thing can I ask for God's help with?*

_____
_____
_____
_____
_____

MORNING

GRATITUDE: *What three things am I thankful for this morning?*

    1. _____

    2. _____

    3. _____

GREATER TRUTH: *What is one absolutely true thing about myself or God?*

_____

_____

_____

_____

_____

GOOD-DAY GRACE: *What is one thing in my control that would make this day a good one?*

_____

_____

_____

_____

EVENING

Who is rich? He who rejoices in his portion.
—BENJAMIN FRANKLIN, QUOTING JEWISH SAGE BEN ZOMA

GRATITUDE: *What are three more things I am thankful for this evening?*

1. _____
2. _____
3. _____

GAFFES: *What one thing would have made today better?*

_____
_____
_____
_____
_____
_____

GOOD-NIGHT GIFT: *What one thing can I ask for God's help with?*

_____
_____
_____
_____
_____

MORNING

DAY 32

—/—/—

GRATITUDE: *What three things am I thankful for this morning?*

1. _____
2. _____
3. _____

GREATER TRUTH: *What is one absolutely true thing about myself or God?*

_____

_____

_____

_____

_____

GOOD-DAY GRACE: *What is one thing in my control that would make this day a good one?*

_____

_____

_____

_____

EVENING

Everything has beauty, but not everyone sees it.

—CONFUCIUS

GRATITUDE: *What are three more things I am thankful for this evening?*

1. _____
2. _____
3. _____

GAFFES: *What one thing would have made today better?*

_____
_____
_____
_____
_____

GOOD-NIGHT GIFT: *What one thing can I ask for God's help with?*

_____
_____
_____
_____
_____

MORNING

GRATITUDE: *What three things am I thankful for this morning?*

1. _____
2. _____
3. _____

GREATER TRUTH: *What is one absolutely true thing about myself or God?*

_____
_____
_____
_____
_____

GOOD-DAY GRACE: *What is one thing in my control that would make this day a good one?*

_____
_____
_____
_____

EVENING

Do few things, but do them well. Simple joys are holy.
— SAINT FRANCIS OF ASSISI

GRATITUDE: *What are three more things I am thankful for this evening?*

1. _____
2. _____
3. _____

GAFFES: *What one thing would have made today better?*

_____
_____
_____
_____
_____

GOOD-NIGHT GIFT: *What one thing can I ask for God's help with?*

_____
_____
_____
_____
_____

MORNING

GRATITUDE: *What three things am I thankful for this morning?*

1. _____
2. _____
3. _____

GREATER TRUTH: *What is one absolutely true thing about myself or God?*

_____
_____
_____
_____
_____

GOOD-DAY GRACE: *What is one thing in my control that would make this day a good one?*

_____
_____
_____

EVENING

Wisdom is not a product of schooling
but of the lifelong attempt to acquire it.
—ALBERT EINSTEIN

GRATITUDE: *What are three more things I am thankful for this evening?*

1. _____
2. _____
3. _____

GAFFES: *What one thing would have made today better?*

_____
_____
_____
_____
_____

GOOD-NIGHT GIFT: *What one thing can I ask for God's help with?*

_____
_____
_____
_____
_____

MORNING

DAY 35

__/__/__

GRATITUDE: *What three things am I thankful for this morning?*

1. _____
2. _____
3. _____

GREATER TRUTH: *What is one absolutely true thing about myself or God?*

_____

_____

_____

_____

_____

GOOD-DAY GRACE: *What is one thing in my control that would make this day a good one?*

_____

_____

_____

_____

EVENING

GRATITUDE: *What are three more things I am thankful for this evening?*

1. _____
2. _____
3. _____

GAFFES: *What one thing would have made today better?*

_____
_____
_____
_____
_____

GOOD-NIGHT GIFT: *What one thing can I ask for God's help with?*

_____
_____
_____
_____
_____

MORNING

GRATITUDE: *What three things am I thankful for this morning?*

    1. _____

    2. _____

    3. _____

GREATER TRUTH: *What is one absolutely true thing about myself or God?*

_____

_____

_____

_____

_____

GOOD-DAY GRACE: *What is one thing in my control that would make this day a good one?*

_____

_____

_____

_____

_____

EVENING

GRATITUDE: *What are three more things I am thankful for this evening?*

1. _____
2. _____
3. _____

GAFFES: *What one thing would have made today better?*

_____
_____
_____
_____
_____

GOOD-NIGHT GIFT: *What one thing can I ask for God's help with?*

_____
_____
_____
_____

MORNING

GRATITUDE: *What three things am I thankful for this morning?*

1. _____
2. _____
3. _____

GREATER TRUTH: *What is one absolutely true thing about myself or God?*

_____

_____

_____

_____

_____

GOOD-DAY GRACE: *What is one thing in my control that would make this day a good one?*

_____

_____

_____

_____

_____

EVENING

*Wherever there is a human being
there is an opportunity for an act of kindness.*
—SENECA

GRATITUDE: *What are three more things I am thankful for this evening?*

1. _____
2. _____
3. _____

GAFFES: *What one thing would have made today better?*

_____
_____
_____
_____
_____

GOOD-NIGHT GIFT: *What one thing can I ask for God's help with?*

_____
_____
_____
_____
_____

MORNING

GRATITUDE: *What three things am I thankful for this morning?*

    1. _____

    2. _____

    3. _____

GREATER TRUTH: *What is one absolutely true thing about myself or God?*

_____

_____

_____

_____

_____

GOOD-DAY GRACE: *What is one thing in my control that would make this day a good one?*

_____

_____

_____

_____

EVENING

Pray as though everything depended on God.
Work as though everything depended on you.

—SAINT AUGUSTINE

GRATITUDE: *What are three more things I am thankful for this evening?*

1. _____
2. _____
3. _____

GAFFES: *What one thing would have made today better?*

_____
_____
_____
_____
_____

GOOD-NIGHT GIFT: *What one thing can I ask for God's help with?*

_____
_____
_____
_____
_____

MORNING

DAY 39

__/__/__

GRATITUDE: *What three things am I thankful for this morning?*

1. _____
2. _____
3. _____

GREATER TRUTH: *What is one absolutely true thing about myself or God?*

_____
_____
_____
_____
_____

GOOD-DAY GRACE: *What is one thing in my control that would make this day a good one?*

_____
_____
_____
_____

EVENING

We need beauty because it makes us ache to be worthy of it.

—MARY OLIVER

GRATITUDE: *What are three more things I am thankful for this evening?*

1. _____
2. _____
3. _____

GAFFES: *What one thing would have made today better?*

_____

_____

_____

_____

GOOD-NIGHT GIFT: *What one thing can I ask for God's help with?*

_____

_____

_____

_____

MORNING

GRATITUDE: *What three things am I thankful for this morning?*

1. _____
2. _____
3. _____

GREATER TRUTH: *What is one absolutely true thing about myself or God?*

_____
_____
_____
_____
_____

GOOD-DAY GRACE: *What is one thing in my control that would make this day a good one?*

_____
_____
_____
_____

EVENING

If we find ourselves with a desire that nothing in this world can satisfy,
the most probable explanation is that we were made for another world.

—C.S. LEWIS

GRATITUDE: *What are three more things I am thankful for this evening?*

1. _____
2. _____
3. _____

GAFFES: *What one thing would have made today better?*

_____

_____

_____

_____

_____

GOOD-NIGHT GIFT: *What one thing can I ask for God's help with?*

_____

_____

_____

_____

_____

MORNING

DAY 41

__/__/__

GRATITUDE: *What three things am I thankful for this morning?*

1. _____
2. _____
3. _____

GREATER TRUTH: *What is one absolutely true thing about myself or God?*

_____
_____
_____
_____
_____

GOOD-DAY GRACE: *What is one thing in my control that would make this day a good one?*

_____
_____
_____
_____
_____

EVENING

I do not feel obliged to believe that the same God who has endowed us with sense, reason, and intellect has intended us to forgo their use.

—GALILEO

GRATITUDE: *What are three more things I am thankful for this evening?*

1. _____
2. _____
3. _____

GAFFES: *What one thing would have made today better?*

_____
_____
_____
_____
_____

GOOD-NIGHT GIFT: *What one thing can I ask for God's help with?*

_____
_____
_____
_____
_____

MORNING

GRATITUDE: *What three things am I thankful for this morning?*

1. _____
2. _____
3. _____

GREATER TRUTH: *What is one absolutely true thing about myself or God?*

_____

_____

_____

_____

GOOD-DAY GRACE: *What is one thing in my control that would make this day a good one?*

_____

_____

_____

_____

EVENING

May you live all the days of your life.
—JONATHAN SWIFT

GRATITUDE: *What are three more things I am thankful for this evening?*

1. _____
2. _____
3. _____

GAFFES: *What one thing would have made today better?*

_____
_____
_____
_____
_____

GOOD-NIGHT GIFT: *What one thing can I ask for God's help with?*

_____
_____
_____
_____

MORNING

GRATITUDE: *What three things am I thankful for this morning?*

1. _____
2. _____
3. _____

GREATER TRUTH: *What is one absolutely true thing about myself or God?*

_____
_____
_____
_____
_____

GOOD-DAY GRACE: *What is one thing in my control that would make this day a good one?*

_____
_____
_____
_____

EVENING

Although the world is full of suffering, it is full also of the overcoming of it.
—HELEN KELLER

GRATITUDE: *What are three more things I am thankful for this evening?*

1. _____
2. _____
3. _____

GAFFES: *What one thing would have made today better?*

_____
_____
_____
_____
_____

GOOD-NIGHT GIFT: *What one thing can I ask for God's help with?*

_____
_____
_____
_____

MORNING

DAY 44

__/__/__

GRATITUDE: *What three things am I thankful for this morning?*

1. _____
2. _____
3. _____

GREATER TRUTH: *What is one absolutely true thing about myself or God?*

_____
_____
_____
_____
_____

GOOD-DAY GRACE: *What is one thing in my control that would make this day a good one?*

_____
_____
_____
_____

EVENING

*The bravest are surely those who have the clearest
vision of what is before them, glory and danger alike, and yet
notwithstanding, go out to meet it.*
—THUCYDIDES

GRATITUDE: *What are three more things I am thankful for this evening?*

1. _____
2. _____
3. _____

GAFFES: *What one thing would have made today better?*

_____
_____
_____
_____
_____

GOOD-NIGHT GIFT: *What one thing can I ask for God's help with?*

_____
_____
_____
_____
_____

MORNING

DAY 45

__/__/__

GRATITUDE: *What three things am I thankful for this morning?*

1. _____
2. _____
3. _____

GREATER TRUTH: *What is one absolutely true thing about myself or God?*

_____
_____
_____
_____
_____

GOOD-DAY GRACE: *What is one thing in my control that would make this day a good one?*

_____
_____
_____
_____

EVENING

Therefore, my beloved, be steadfast, immovable,
always excelling in the work of the Lord, because you know
that in the Lord your labor is not in vain.

—1 CORINTHIANS 15:58

GRATITUDE: *What are three more things I am thankful for this evening?*

1. _____
2. _____
3. _____

GAFFES: *What one thing would have made today better?*

_____
_____
_____
_____
_____

GOOD-NIGHT GIFT: *What one thing can I ask for God's help with?*

_____
_____
_____
_____
_____

MORNING

DAY 46

___/___/___

GRATITUDE: *What three things am I thankful for this morning?*

1. _____
2. _____
3. _____

GREATER TRUTH: *What is one absolutely true thing about myself or God?*

_____
_____
_____
_____
_____

GOOD-DAY GRACE: *What is one thing in my control that would make this day a good one?*

_____
_____
_____
_____

EVENING

May today there be peace within. May you trust
God that you are exactly where you are meant to be.
—SAINT TERESA OF AVILA

GRATITUDE: *What are three more things I am thankful for this evening?*

1. _____
2. _____
3. _____

GAFFES: *What one thing would have made today better?*

_____
_____
_____
_____
_____

GOOD-NIGHT GIFT: *What one thing can I ask for God's help with?*

_____
_____
_____
_____

MORNING

DAY 47

__/__/__

GRATITUDE: *What three things am I thankful for this morning?*

1. _____
2. _____
3. _____

GREATER TRUTH: *What is one absolutely true thing about myself or God?*

_____
_____
_____
_____
_____

GOOD-DAY GRACE: *What is one thing in my control that would make this day a good one?*

_____
_____
_____
_____
_____

EVENING

*Happiness depends more upon the internal frame of
a person's own mind than on the externals in the world.*
—GEORGE WASHINGTON

GRATITUDE: *What are three more things I am thankful for this evening?*

1. _____
2. _____
3. _____

GAFFES: *What one thing would have made today better?*

_____
_____
_____
_____
_____

GOOD-NIGHT GIFT: *What one thing can I ask for God's help with?*

_____
_____
_____
_____

MORNING

DAY 48

__ / __ / __

GRATITUDE: *What three things am I thankful for this morning?*

1. _____
2. _____
3. _____

GREATER TRUTH: *What is one absolutely true thing about myself or God?*

_____
_____
_____
_____
_____

GOOD-DAY GRACE: *What is one thing in my control that would make this day a good one?*

_____
_____
_____
_____

EVENING

It is not the critic who counts; not the man who points out how the strong man stumbles, or where the doer of deeds could have done them better. The credit belongs to the man who is actually in the arena.

—THEODORE ROOSEVELT

GRATITUDE: *What are three more things I am thankful for this evening?*

1. _____
2. _____
3. _____

GAFFES: *What one thing would have made today better?*

_____
_____
_____
_____
_____

GOOD-NIGHT GIFT: *What one thing can I ask for God's help with?*

_____
_____
_____
_____
_____

MORNING

DAY 49

__/__/__

GRATITUDE: *What three things am I thankful for this morning?*

1. _____
2. _____
3. _____

GREATER TRUTH: *What is one absolutely true thing about myself or God?*

_____
_____
_____
_____
_____

GOOD-DAY GRACE: *What is one thing in my control that would make this day a good one?*

_____
_____
_____
_____
_____

EVENING

GRATITUDE: *What are three more things I am thankful for this evening?*

1. _____
2. _____
3. _____

GAFFES: *What one thing would have made today better?*

_____
_____
_____
_____
_____

GOOD-NIGHT GIFT: *What one thing can I ask for God's help with?*

_____
_____
_____
_____
_____

MORNING

DAY 50

__/__/__

GRATITUDE: *What three things am I thankful for this morning?*

1. _____
2. _____
3. _____

GREATER TRUTH: *What is one absolutely true thing about myself or God?*

_____
_____
_____
_____
_____

GOOD-DAY GRACE: *What is one thing in my control that would make this day a good one?*

_____
_____
_____
_____

EVENING

*[God] will either give us what we ask, or what
He knows to be better for us.*
—SAINT BERNARD OF CLAIRVAUX

GRATITUDE: *What are three more things I am thankful for this evening?*

1. _____
2. _____
3. _____

GAFFES: *What one thing would have made today better?*

_____
_____
_____
_____
_____

GOOD-NIGHT GIFT: *What one thing can I ask for God's help with?*

_____
_____
_____
_____
_____

MORNING

GRATITUDE: *What three things am I thankful for this morning?*

1. _____
2. _____
3. _____

GREATER TRUTH: *What is one absolutely true thing about myself or God?*

_____
_____
_____
_____

GOOD-DAY GRACE: *What is one thing in my control that would make this day a good one?*

_____
_____
_____
_____

EVENING

Life shrinks or expands in proportion to one's courage.

—ANAIS NIN

GRATITUDE: *What are three more things I am thankful for this evening?*

1. _____
2. _____
3. _____

GAFFES: *What one thing would have made today better?*

_____
_____
_____
_____
_____

GOOD-NIGHT GIFT: *What one thing can I ask for God's help with?*

_____
_____
_____
_____

MORNING

GRATITUDE: *What three things am I thankful for this morning?*

1. _____
2. _____
3. _____

GREATER TRUTH: *What is one absolutely true thing about myself or God?*

_____
_____
_____
_____
_____

GOOD-DAY GRACE: *What is one thing in my control that would make this day a good one?*

_____
_____
_____
_____
_____

EVENING

GRATITUDE: *What are three more things I am thankful for this evening?*

1. _____
2. _____
3. _____

GAFFES: *What one thing would have made today better?*

_____
_____
_____
_____
_____
_____

GOOD-NIGHT GIFT: *What one thing can I ask for God's help with?*

_____
_____
_____
_____
_____

MORNING

GRATITUDE: *What three things am I thankful for this morning?*

1. _____
2. _____
3. _____

GREATER TRUTH: *What is one absolutely true thing about myself or God?*

_____
_____
_____
_____
_____

GOOD-DAY GRACE: *What is one thing in my control that would make this day a good one?*

_____
_____
_____
_____

EVENING

God's work, done in God's way, will never lack God's supplies.
—HUDSON TAYLOR

GRATITUDE: *What are three more things I am thankful for this evening?*

1. _____
2. _____
3. _____

GAFFES: *What one thing would have made today better?*

_____

_____

_____

_____

_____

GOOD-NIGHT GIFT: *What one thing can I ask for God's help with?*

_____

_____

_____

_____

_____

MORNING

DAY 54

__/__/__

GRATITUDE: *What three things am I thankful for this morning?*

1. _____
2. _____
3. _____

GREATER TRUTH: *What is one absolutely true thing about myself or God?*

_____

_____

_____

_____

GOOD-DAY GRACE: *What is one thing in my control that would make this day a good one?*

_____

_____

_____

EVENING

To do the useful thing, to say the courageous thing, to contemplate the beautiful thing: that is enough for one man's life.

—T.S. ELIOT

GRATITUDE: *What are three more things I am thankful for this evening?*

1. _____
2. _____
3. _____

GAFFES: *What one thing would have made today better?*

_____
_____
_____
_____
_____

GOOD-NIGHT GIFT: *What one thing can I ask for God's help with?*

_____
_____
_____
_____
_____

GRATITUDE: *What three things am I thankful for this morning?*

1. _____
2. _____
3. _____

GREATER TRUTH: *What is one absolutely true thing about myself or God?*

_____
_____
_____
_____
_____

GOOD-DAY GRACE: *What is one thing in my control that would make this day a good one?*

_____
_____
_____
_____

EVENING

You gain strength, courage and confidence by every experience in which you really stop to look fear in the face.
—ELEANOR ROOSEVELT

GRATITUDE: *What are three more things I am thankful for this evening?*

1. _____
2. _____
3. _____

GAFFES: *What one thing would have made today better?*

_____
_____
_____
_____
_____

GOOD-NIGHT GIFT: *What one thing can I ask for God's help with?*

_____
_____
_____
_____
_____

MORNING

DAY 56

__/__/__

GRATITUDE: *What three things am I thankful for this morning?*

1. _____
2. _____
3. _____

GREATER TRUTH: *What is one absolutely true thing about myself or God?*

_____
_____
_____
_____
_____

GOOD-DAY GRACE: *What is one thing in my control that would make this day a good one?*

_____
_____
_____
_____

EVENING

Live as if you were to die tomorrow; learn as if you were to live forever.
—MAHATMA GANDHI

GRATITUDE: *What are three more things I am thankful for this evening?*

1. _____
2. _____
3. _____

GAFFES: *What one thing would have made today better?*

_____
_____
_____
_____
_____

GOOD-NIGHT GIFT: *What one thing can I ask for God's help with?*

_____
_____
_____
_____
_____

MORNING

GRATITUDE: *What three things am I thankful for this morning?*

1. _____
2. _____
3. _____

GREATER TRUTH: *What is one absolutely true thing about myself or God?*

_____

_____

_____

_____

GOOD-DAY GRACE: *What is one thing in my control that would make this day a good one?*

_____

_____

_____

_____

EVENING

Life is entrusted to man as a treasure which must not be squandered,
as a talent which must be used well.

—SAINT JOHN PAUL II

GRATITUDE: *What are three more things I am thankful for this evening?*

1. _____
2. _____
3. _____

GAFFES: *What one thing would have made today better?*

_____
_____
_____
_____

GOOD-NIGHT GIFT: *What one thing can I ask for God's help with?*

_____
_____
_____
_____
_____

MORNING

GRATITUDE: *What three things am I thankful for this morning?*

1. _____
2. _____
3. _____

GREATER TRUTH: *What is one absolutely true thing about myself or God?*

_____
_____
_____
_____
_____

GOOD-DAY GRACE: *What is one thing in my control that would make this day a good one?*

_____
_____
_____
_____

EVENING

To live will be an awfully big adventure.
—J.M. BARRIE

GRATITUDE: *What are three more things I am thankful for this evening?*

1. _____
2. _____
3. _____

GAFFES: *What one thing would have made today better?*

_____
_____
_____
_____
_____

GOOD-NIGHT GIFT: *What one thing can I ask for God's help with?*

_____
_____
_____
_____
_____

MORNING

DAY 59

__/__/__

GRATITUDE: *What three things am I thankful for this morning?*

1. _____
2. _____
3. _____

GREATER TRUTH: *What is one absolutely true thing about myself or God?*

_____
_____
_____
_____

GOOD-DAY GRACE: *What is one thing in my control that would make this day a good one?*

_____
_____
_____
_____

EVENING

Miracles in fact are a retelling in small letters of the very same story which is written across the whole world in letters too large for some of us to see.

—C.S. LEWIS

GRATITUDE: *What are three more things I am thankful for this evening?*

1. _____
2. _____
3. _____

GAFFES: *What one thing would have made today better?*

_____
_____
_____
_____
_____

GOOD-NIGHT GIFT: *What one thing can I ask for God's help with?*

_____
_____
_____
_____
_____

MORNING

DAY 60

___/___/___

GRATITUDE: *What three things am I thankful for this morning?*

1. _____
2. _____
3. _____

GREATER TRUTH: *What is one absolutely true thing about myself or God?*

_____
_____
_____
_____
_____

GOOD-DAY GRACE: *What is one thing in my control that would make this day a good one?*

_____
_____
_____
_____

EVENING

Trust in the LORD with all your heart, and do not lean on your own understanding. In all your ways acknowledge him, and he will make straight your paths.

—PROVERBS 3:5-6 ESV

GRATITUDE: *What are three more things I am thankful for this evening?*

1. _____
2. _____
3. _____

GAFFES: *What one thing would have made today better?*

_____
_____
_____
_____
_____

GOOD-NIGHT GIFT: *What one thing can I ask for God's help with?*

_____
_____
_____
_____
_____

MORNING

GRATITUDE: *What three things am I thankful for this morning?*

1. _____
2. _____
3. _____

GREATER TRUTH: *What is one absolutely true thing about myself or God?*

_____
_____
_____
_____
_____

GOOD-DAY GRACE: *What is one thing in my control that would make this day a good one?*

_____
_____
_____
_____

EVENING

'No one is more unhappy, in my judgment . . . than a man who has never met with adversity.' He has never had the privilege of testing himself.
—SENECA, QUOTING HIS FRIEND DEMETRIUS

GRATITUDE: *What are three more things I am thankful for this evening?*

1. _____
2. _____
3. _____

GAFFES: *What one thing would have made today better?*

_____
_____
_____
_____
_____

GOOD-NIGHT GIFT: *What one thing can I ask for God's help with?*

_____
_____
_____
_____
_____

MORNING

DAY 62

__/__/__

GRATITUDE: *What three things am I thankful for this morning?*

1. _____
2. _____
3. _____

GREATER TRUTH: *What is one absolutely true thing about myself or God?*

_____
_____
_____
_____
_____

GOOD-DAY GRACE: *What is one thing in my control that would make this day a good one?*

_____
_____
_____
_____

EVENING

The most difficult thing is the decision to act, the rest is merely tenacity.

—AMELIA EARHART

GRATITUDE: *What are three more things I am thankful for this evening?*

1. _____
2. _____
3. _____

GAFFES: *What one thing would have made today better?*

_____

_____

_____

_____

_____

GOOD-NIGHT GIFT: *What one thing can I ask for God's help with?*

_____

_____

_____

_____

_____

MORNING

GRATITUDE: *What three things am I thankful for this morning?*

1. _____
2. _____
3. _____

GREATER TRUTH: *What is one absolutely true thing about myself or God?*

_____

_____

_____

_____

_____

GOOD-DAY GRACE: *What is one thing in my control that would make this day a good one?*

_____

_____

_____

_____

EVENING

There is no saint without a past, no sinner without a future.
—ATTRIBUTED TO SAINT AUGUSTINE

GRATITUDE: *What are three more things I am thankful for this evening?*

1. _____
2. _____
3. _____

GAFFES: *What one thing would have made today better?*

_____
_____
_____
_____
_____

GOOD-NIGHT GIFT: *What one thing can I ask for God's help with?*

_____
_____
_____
_____
_____

MORNING

DAY 64

__/__/__

GRATITUDE: *What three things am I thankful for this morning?*

1. _____
2. _____
3. _____

GREATER TRUTH: *What is one absolutely true thing about myself or God?*

_____

_____

_____

_____

_____

GOOD-DAY GRACE: *What is one thing in my control that would make this day a good one?*

_____

_____

_____

_____

_____

EVENING

Life can only be understood backwards; but it must be lived forwards.

—SØREN KIERKEGAARD

GRATITUDE: *What are three more things I am thankful for this evening?*

1. _____
2. _____
3. _____

GAFFES: *What one thing would have made today better?*

_____
_____
_____
_____
_____

GOOD-NIGHT GIFT: *What one thing can I ask for God's help with?*

_____
_____
_____
_____
_____

MORNING

GRATITUDE: *What three things am I thankful for this morning?*

1. _____
2. _____
3. _____

GREATER TRUTH: *What is one absolutely true thing about myself or God?*

_____
_____
_____
_____
_____

GOOD-DAY GRACE: *What is one thing in my control that would make this day a good one?*

_____
_____
_____
_____

EVENING

Yesterday I was clever, so I wanted to change the world.
Today I am wise, so I am changing myself.

—RUMI

GRATITUDE: *What are three more things I am thankful for this evening?*

1. _____
2. _____
3. _____

GAFFES: *What one thing would have made today better?*

_____
_____
_____
_____
_____

GOOD-NIGHT GIFT: *What one thing can I ask for God's help with?*

_____
_____
_____
_____
_____

CONCLUSION

Socrates once quipped, "The unexamined life is not worth living." While we may never find ourselves in Ancient Greece on trial for impiety and corrupting youth, we would do well to take heed of Socrates's learned wisdom. I'd argue that with the daily ink marks you've made in this journal, you're taking his advice by examining your life. You're noticing the big and small moments that make up your days, and you're acknowledging that they're not for nothing. It may seem minor to you, but your small practice of marking the first light and eventide of each day is actually quite monumental. In doing so, you're saying that the day mattered. You're declaring that your life, no matter how small, is full of intricacies planned before the foundations of the world and that your choices make a difference in your corner of that world. Well done.

Though nobody can go back and make a new beginning, anyone can start over and make a new ending.
—CHICO XAVIER

Done is better than perfect, of course. It's okay if you had days you skipped or days you scribbled down whatever was easiest. Hopefully, you've not intended to fill this journal for the sole purpose of creating a museum-worthy artifact. My prayer is that your time in these pages served as an Ebenezer for you, a reminder to help you recognize the hand of God in your life. If it did, I invite you to keep up your practice. Make this morning and evening Examen a lifelong habit. Decide to etch these six questions in stone as permanent bookmarks that stand as bulwarks to your waking hours. You'll never regret taking five minutes to notice your day and to place in your pocket a sliver of wisdom from our elders of the ages.

Even if you're on the right track, you'll get run over if you just sit there.

—WILL ROGERS

WHAT IS THE USE OF LIVING, IF IT
BE NOT TO STRIVE FOR NOBLE CAUSES
AND MAKE THIS MUDDLED WORLD
A BETTER PLACE FOR THOSE WHO WILL
LIVE IN IT AFTER WE ARE GONE?

—*Winston Churchill*

BENEDICTION

A benediction is a blessing spoken over an individual or group of people before they go on their way. The word's etymology stems from Latin: *bene* meaning "good" and *dicere* meaning "say." A benediction is a literal good word given from one person to another with the intention that God would bless the words with the infused grace needed for them to come to fruition.

> *Earth's crammed with heaven,*
> *and every common bush afire*
> *with God, but only he who sees*
> *takes off his shoes, the rest sit*
> *round it and pluck blackberries.*
> —ELIZABETH BARRETT BROWNING

With this in mind, I'd be honored to bless your intentions, ideas, and observations you've collected in this journal. Your scribbles represent your morning and evening bookends that have made up your quotidian, extraordinary ordinary life. May I never presume to do more than consecrate your days as a companion along the way, here with this simple benediction that I say heartily for the both of us:

Fellow pilgrim,

May the words you've captured between these covers acknowledge

    in your heart, eyes, and mind

the truest goodness and beauty that lives.

May your etchings remind you what's real, what's honorable, what's

    longing to be remembered as you live the commonplaceness of your day.

May the simple but sacred practice of noticing

the things that are more real than the tangible around you

open your soul to receive eternal truth about who you really are,

that it will reveal what matters more than the here and now.

May you notice pilgrim companions around you,

may you point out the view as you follow the road's bends,

and may you nod in quiet agreement when they do likewise with you.

May you remember to walk the road equipped with essentials:

Water and a good night's sleep and sturdy shoes, yes,

but also with a determination to find glory in the mundane,

curiosity in the common,

and a submission to the democracy of the dead,

infusing your modern life with sagacity of those who've walked before.

May your life be extraordinarily ordinary

so that you never despise the daily work of your hands

nor ever ignore the awe of an apple.

May you always remove your shoes at the blackberry bush.

God be with you as you go.

Tsh Oxenreider is a bestselling author as well as a teacher, travel guide, and podcaster. Her books include *Shadow and Light* and *Bitter and Sweet*. Tsh's popular weekly newsletter reaches tens of thousands of loyal readers. Tsh and her family have traveled the world and lived all over but are currently happy to call Central Texas home.

Unless otherwise indicated, all Scripture quotations are taken from the New Revised Standard Version Bible, copyright © 1989 National Council of the Churches of Christ in the United States of America. Used by permission. All rights reserved worldwide.

Scripture quotations marked NLT are taken from the Holy Bible, New Living Translation, copyright © 1996, 2004, 2015 by Tyndale House Foundation. Used by permission of Tyndale House Publishers, Inc., Carol Stream, Illinois 60188. All rights reserved.

Verses marked NIV are taken from the Holy Bible, New International Version®, NIV®. Copyright © 1973, 1978, 1984, 2011 by Biblica, Inc.® Used by permission of Zondervan. All rights reserved worldwide. www.zondervan.com. The "NIV" and "New International Version" are trademarks registered in the United States Patent and Trademark Office by Biblica, Inc.®

Verses marked HCSB have been taken from the Holman Christian Standard Bible®, Used by permission © 1999, 2000, 2002, 2003, 2009 Holman Bible Publishers. Holman Christian Standard Bible®, Holman CSB®, and HCSB® are federally registered trademarks of Holman Bible Publishers.

Verses marked ESV are taken from the ESV® Bible (The Holy Bible, English Standard Version®), copyright © 2001 by Crossway, a publishing ministry of Good News Publishers. Used by permission. All rights reserved.

Published in association with Jenni Burke of Illuminate Literary Agency: www.illuminateliterary.com

Cover design, interior design, and illustrations by Connie Gabbert Design and Illustration

This logo is a federally registered trademark of the Hawkins Children's LLC. Harvest House Publishers, Inc., is the exclusive licensee of this trademark.

First Light and Eventide
Copyright © 2023 by Tsh Oxenreider
Published by Harvest House Publishers
Eugene, Oregon 97408
www.harvesthousepublishers.com

ISBN 978-0-7369-8710-3 (hardcover)

Printed in China

23 24 25 26 27 28 29 30 31 /RDS—CG/ 10 9 8 7 6 5 4 3 2 1